Sa,

May true
peace
and
happiness
always
follow
you!
Victor

THE 16 JOY PRINCIPLES
OF LIVING! (AND OTHER
INSPIRATIONAL WRITINGS :)

Victor Cyr
Hamilton,Ontario. Canada

victorcyr@gmail.com

Dedicated to the God of my life and for all he has taught me through it.

Table of Contents:

Introduction

Don't we all strive to live daily a life of love, joy, peace and contentment?

Strangely it seems though that life's changing circumstances often appear to conspire against us, making it very difficult for anyone to find this utopian place of goodness in a consistent manner.

However, could it be that it's not the vicissitudes of life that is the problem, but simply how we view them and the attitudes we form to try to cope with the hardships they inevitably bring?

It was the great Greek philosopher Epictetus who once said, "Men are disturbed not by things, but by the view which they take of them." How true that is for such a large part of the human family!

The overriding purpose of this short book is to help foster good and positive thoughts about our existence which happens on the three planes of our lives: the physical, the emotional/mental, and the spiritual, all aspects of who we truly are in our human essence.

It is my hope and wish that you may find something in these writings that speaks to who you are in the deepest part of your personality.

These insights have been born out of my own challenges and trials, as they usually are for most people who end up finding something of great significance for themselves from the inevitable difficulties and sufferings that come their way.

Hopefully you can point to these things and say, "Yes, this is truly real for me and yes, these are some principles I can live by to make my life joyous regardless of the circumstances before me."

May you rise to new heights of self-discovery and inner happiness as you venture through these writings, meditate on them, apply them to your own personal situations and witness the changes that will come as you begin to view your life from a surprisingly different perspective.

Principle # 1:

So often we wish our lives were being lived out differently than what they presently are.........relationships that fail and are no longer part of who we are, work opportunities squandered or lost, family situations that didn't turn out the way we had hoped, lingering health concerns and the list can go on and on.

Yet accepting all these situations unconditionally, without regret or remorse for the sole purpose of teaching us something very important on how to live our lives better, can go a long way to helping us to both achieve and maintain our peace of mind in all circumstances.

Joy principle thought to ponder and embrace:

If we take every situation and circumstance in life as they are presented to us and not as we wish them to be, there in due course we can find peace, joy and wisdom beyond compare.

Every good thing that comes our way gives us reason to rejoice and be happy, while every difficult and trying event gives us the opportunity to grow in strength, wisdom, character and perseverance that most good-time circumstances can never teach us.

Ultimately everything in life can work for our good if we just shake it down to its ultimate reality and see it for what it really is.

My personal reflection on this principle:

_____

_____

_____

_____

_____

Principle # 2:

Self-love is often times a misunderstood concept among a lot of people. It conjures up images of narcissism, arrogance, and a host of other unsavory character attributes that can turn others off.

Yet true self-love is rooted in humility and a wonderful inner feeling from a belief system that one's life counts; that we along with all others are worthy of dignity and self-respect just because of who we are in the grand scheme of things.

As we endeavor to see and accept ourselves from that wonderful vantage point, we can then go out each day and share that same self-affirming love to those whose spirits are burdened by low self-esteem or self-loathing.

Joy principle thought to ponder and embrace:

Endeavor to be kind and compassionate to everyone you meet, both friend and foe alike.

However, to have the capacity and authenticity to do that means we need to first extend those same attributes to ourselves.

It doesn't matter if we are succeeding or failing, feeling good or not so great....be kind and compassionate to ourselves in everything and experience the joy of the unconditional acceptance of our true humanity.

After all, a person can only give away to others what they themselves possess.

My personal reflection on this principle:

_____

_____

_____

_____

_____

Principle # 3:

The kind of words and conversations we share with others in the run of a day is usually a good barometer of what is going on in our own minds and hearts.

It seems the self-dialogue we often have with ourselves can be slanted to the negative side of our personalities unless we consciously stop and re-shape those errant thoughts to reflect a more positive and loving approach to both ourselves and others.

This form of self-discipline in our thinking often requires much hard work and a willingness to stay with the program until the habit gets established.

Some mental health professionals tell us that we have five seconds to alter a thought to make it conform to what we want it to be before it resides in our subconscious mind and it becomes a part of our mindset.

Joy principle thought to ponder and embrace:

We often times don't stop to think of the powerful effect that words have both on ourselves and others.

Everyday a self-dialogue goes on in our minds forming thoughts that will ultimately express themselves in our words and actions.

To manage this part of our lives well, each of us must establish a value system that monitors objectively this stream of consciousness that lies within us all, weeding out the destructive self-talk and bringing to the forefront of our thinking and speaking all that is positive, loving and good.

My personal reflection on this principle:

_____

_____

_____

_____

_____

Principle # 4:

Most people in life want to appear to themselves and others as competent, capable individuals who are worthy of respect because of their wise actions and words.

Yet the reality of mistakes, miscues, and misjudgments in our lives and in the lives of others that happen from time to time can war against those feelings of being seen as consistent people of reliability and strong substance.

However, keeping a realistic and positive attitude about our imperfections will guard against feelings of low-self-esteem and self-condemnation whenever we feel we have missed the mark in achieving the level of competency we desire to reach in life.

Joy principle thought to ponder and embrace:

When it comes to our serious mistakes or failures in life there are two general approaches a person can take:

One is to beat ourselves up over them and live perpetually in guilt, shame, and regret.

The other is to look at these setbacks as experience-gathering exercises that will serve us well for future endeavors in life.

The former attitude will ultimately wreck us emotionally and spiritually if left unchallenged, while the latter attitude will enrich our understanding of how life really works, leading us to a greater state of intelligence and a personality steeped in wisdom, humility, and transparency.

My personal reflection on this principle:

_____

_____

_____

_____

_____

Principle # 5:

Other than the death of a loved one, there is perhaps nothing harder to accept in life than being rejected by someone who we value a great deal.

Whenever we pour all our love and emotional energy into an individual or entity of some type only to see us rebuffed in return, the resulting feelings of loss can sometimes cause significant mental trauma if we do not frame those situations from a proper perspective.

Joy principle thought to ponder and embrace:

To keep our inner peace intact at all times we need to accept fully a person's choice to reject us as much as we are happy when someone we have affection/admiration for accepts us.

If from the rejection of others toward us we had acted honorably in that relationship than the issue of non-acceptance is not ours to stress over.

Therefore, we can move on in peace, perhaps somewhat temporarily, emotionally wounded from that encounter, but with our dignity, confidence, and self-worth still firmly intact.

If it was our actions that caused the rejection to come about, then it is our responsibility to make amends and apologies where necessary and move on using that experience as a catalyst for a better "me" in future relationships.

My personal reflection on this principle:

_____

_____

_____

_____

_____

Principle # 6:

How we wish at times that we had the power to make the whole world right when we see or read of some injustice that has harmed others in one way or another.

Reality tells us, however, that none of us have the ability to right all wrongs, but we all have the power to work for good in the area of influence that we have been placed in, and that is all that is required of us.

It makes no sense to just throw up our hands and say, "It's no use, the world is beyond fixing!" Instead, let each of us be passionate about changing what we can, where we can, when we can.

By so doing, we will find a great change happen within ourselves as we engage the world from the perspective of being our brother's keeper.

Joy principle thought to ponder and embrace:

It is readily apparent that the world we live in is full of trouble that is not all of our own making and far beyond any one person's ability to fix by themselves.

Therefore, from a compassionate standpoint, it stands to reason that every responsible human being must do their part to help right some wrong that exists, things that rob others of their dignity and self-worth.

Paradoxically, in so finding and living out with passion our desire to help others in their troubles, we mysteriously find a great part of our own self-worth and dignity in the process.

This is one thing that makes life truly worth living and the high purpose that each person is called to seek in the one opportunity we have to live here on this earth.

My personal reflection on this principle:

_____

_____

_____

_____

_____

Principle # 7:

When it comes to trying to understand the concept of God or the divine presence within the universe there are a multitude of opinions on what this may look like.

Some have the perception of a harsh, judgmental entity at work while others believe this eternal, creative force must be benevolent in nature instead.

I choose to believe in a God who has as his base nature the spirit of love, joy, peace, compassion, goodness, and strength. Admittedly, however, many of us struggle with understanding why so much evil and hatred exists in our world if God indeed has these high attributes and can do something about all that is wrong.

Perhaps some things are meant to remain a mystery for now and each person is simply called to explore the nature of goodness and faith within ourselves as placed there by our Creator. We can then let these things shine forth in our everyday human interaction with others wherever we live, move, and make our presence known until our end comes.

Joy principle thought to ponder and embrace:

God in his essence is love, joy, peace, compassion, goodness and strength....what he is each of us should desire to be if we want fullness of life and true happiness in our human experience.

To genuinely possess these six great qualities among others, we should ask him the moment upon waking to fill us with this kind of power, and then with his Spirit to guide us, share it with everyone you make contact with throughout the day.

It is in doing this that we find an unalterable true connection to our authentic selves and to others.

My personal reflection on this principle:

_____

_____

_____

_____

_____

Principle # 8:

Have you ever heard other people say, "When I retire I will finally be able to enjoy all the things I want to do?" Or, maybe we've heard people say, "When I get financially solvent," or "When my health improves," etc.

It's funny how we humans tend to put off to tomorrow what we should be doing today, and none more so than those waiting for a better day to arrive rather than living fully in the here and now and making each day count no matter what shape it takes.

Joy principle thought to ponder and embrace:

One of the biggest deceptions we tell ourselves is that life can't really be enjoyed to the full unless it is free of pressing problems and strong challenges.

However, it is those very things that make life interesting and push us to the fullness of our capacity to work on overcoming them.

Once done, we feel a sense of accomplishment and strength that ushers within us a deep sense of meaning and purpose that no pleasurable, easy life experience could ever provide.

My personal reflection on this principle:

_____

_____

_____

_____

_____

Principle # 9:

Change. Oh, the fears and worries it sometimes brings into our lives when we least want it!

What is it we most fear however about change you would say? No doubt the one big obstacle is the dread of the unknown, of not being totally in the know about what will happen next and how it will affect us and those closest to us.

Reality, however, tells us that everything eventually changes. With this certainty before us, the only healthy approach to this high-level of living is to welcome change with open arms whether we institute it ourselves or it is foisted upon us by circumstances beyond our control.

Joy principle thought to ponder and embrace:

We are all designed to grow in one form or another in our lives, but moving ahead and accomplishing our dreams is at times a demanding task.

No growth comes however without change and a conscious willingness to allow ourselves to be stretched past our present comfort zones, whatever they may be.

Therefore, we should always be willing to bite off a bit more than we can chew, but not so much that it causes us to choke.

It is this healthy, balanced approach to growth that will yield results in the long run.

My personal reflection on this principle:

_____

_____

_____

_____

_____

Principle # 10:

Taste, touch, smell, seeing and hearing are the five basic senses that most of us possess. More often than not, we rely exclusively on them for how we view reality and come to the decisions we will ultimately make.

However, faith as the Christian scriptures attest to is, "Being sure of what we hope for and certain of what we do not see." Hebrews.11:1-NIV.

It is the profound understanding deep in the caverns of our souls, that there is far more to life than what the physical senses are telling us.

That somehow, on another plane which we cannot presently comprehend, something magnificent and eternal is being shaped from our everyday human interaction within ourselves and with others.

Joy principle thought to ponder and embrace:

Faith being the belief in something that cannot be detected by the physical senses alone grants us entry into the realm of the supernatural and into the things that presently remain unseen.

The future is unseen yet we believe it will still come in one form or another into our reality.

This faith, however, doesn't have to be blind or lacking in credibility to be real. We instinctively know it to be true, therefore we wait in eager expectation for its manifestation to take hold in our lives either in this present world or in the world which is yet to come.

My personal reflection on this principle:

_____

_____

_____

_____

_____

Principle # 11:

It is amazing how much time in the run of a typical day the average person will spend thinking or perhaps even brooding over something that has happened in the past.

We have all wished for the ability to go back and change something that we did incorrectly or to prevent a wrong committed against us. Some of us would like to re-capture once again a pleasant circumstance that brought us so much happiness and joy.

Yet an unhealthy fixation with our past can be detrimental to our forward progress in true, present-day living.

Therefore, we must view those previous encounters from a perspective that keeps us emotionally and spiritually balanced as we venture headlong into the unknown.

Joy principle thought to ponder and embrace:

Our past experiences are simply now a collection of memories but they can still serve a useful purpose to us here in this present time.

Former joyful times can bring a smile to our faces, knowing that we once experienced such wonderful moments of elation, while previous tough situations help to form in us wisdom principles that will assist us in living well in the here-and-now and into the future.

Don't discount today the full value of our past experiences – we are the sum total of all of them!

My personal reflection on this principle:

_____

_____

_____

_____

_____

Principle # 12:

The power of choice is an attribute that appears to belong exclusively to us humans and one of the defining traits that separate us from all other forms of life.

We erroneously conclude at times that this power to choose what we want and how to think is without impediment, but often our choices are influenced by how we were raised and the internal emotional/mental filters that were formed because of this profound nurturing element in our lives.

Nonetheless, for those of sane mind, those same filters can be altered to conform to the value system we choose to live by at this present time, thereby giving us the power to help shape what our future will look like.

Joy principle thought to ponder and embrace:

Everyday our lives are full of choices we must make....some are rather mundane and some may be life changing, but they nonetheless must still be made depending on the circumstances before us.

All of us are free, of course, to make any choice we wish, but none of us are free to determine the consequences of those choices.

Those outcomes have already been established based on societal norms and unalterable physical and spiritual laws.

Therefore, we must treat this part of our lives with sober judgement and penetrating insight.

My personal reflection on this principle:

_____

_____

_____

_____

_____

Principle # 13:

Most everyone deals with the troubling emotion of guilt at some point in their lives (unless they suffer from some form of mental illness that doesn't allow them to experience this kind of feeling).

Quite frequently guilt can cause people to engage in some form of irrational action in order to soothe their consciences, or it can make a person emotionally sick as one fixates on something one may have said or did that injured another person or thing.

Yet, when processed correctly in our lives, guilt can spur us on to deal with our past in a healthy way and set us free from those nagging, lingering feelings that we cannot be forgiven for what we have done.

Joy principle thought to embrace and ponder:

Guilt is an emotion that can act as a double-edge sword in our lives.

It can rightly spur us on to correct our wrongful actions that may have caused injury to ourselves or others, or it can debilitate our psychological/ spiritual well-being by making us feel responsible for things not of our own doing or beyond our ability to control.

The key here is to be able to discern between these two forms of guilt in the human experience and deal with them in such a way that our growth in right-living is enhanced every day.

To be able to discern the one from the other, we need to cultivate a life of self-reflection and honest insight into who we genuinely are in our value system of belief and how others interact with us and us with them.

By so doing, the things of life over time begin to appear to us with clarity and understanding and we can then move forward handling this powerful emotion in a correct and healthy way.

My personal reflection on this principle:

_____

_____

_____

_____

_____

Principle # 14:

The word "legacy" is one that takes on a greater meaning in our lives as we grow older and move closer to the finish line of our earthly existence.

So many look back with regret for things they wished they had done while still able to do so, while others wish they had not done certain things that diminished their standing and reputation among loved ones.

Both of these things are ultimately derived from one's choices in life, therefore, it is incumbent upon every person to think carefully before acting as our choices often shape much of our destiny.

Joy principle thought to ponder and embrace:

Some people go through life leaving behind them a trail of destruction, tears and pain for others to bear while some others live passionately to alleviate human suffering wherever it may be found.

The former are primarily driven by the desire to fulfill their own needs/ego while the latter are often spurred on by their altruistic desire to make the world a better place, or because of their faith in God.

We all get to choose each day what way to live regardless of the previous forces and influences that have shaped our lives up to this present moment.

My personal reflection on this principle:

_____

_____

_____

_____

_____

Principle # 15:

Never before in the course of human history have we had so much knowledge and information at our disposal.

Literally, "We have the world at our fingertips", and so with it comes a double-edge sword of both benefit and possible negative consequences.

Losing our ability to reflect on what we ingest due to time constraints or the sheer mass of data we try to process too quickly can lead to rushed, harried lives devoid of peace, joy and the satisfaction that comes with cultivating genuine, personal relationships with others.

Striking the right balance between sufficient knowledge gathering and taking the time to nurture critical, life-affirming relationships will be the test for the next generation to live out.

Joy principle thought to ponder and embrace:

With the onslaught of information that is before us today it is easy to start letting go of the practice of taking time to reflect and ponder what it is we are actually reading, or to cultivate close personal relationships that can bring so much joy to our human experience.

When we simply absorb information for information's sake and don't think deeply of the messages we ingest into our minds and spirits, we can lose touch with that part of our lives that enables us to feel and experience the power of words and their influence in our lives.

We can also forget how the loss of the power of those same words may negatively impact the lives of those we may interact with on a daily basis.

My personal reflection on this principle:

_____

_____

_____

_____

_____

Principle #16:

As a child growing up I had a morbid fear of death after losing a good friend at the young age of seven in a car accident…. one day he was here and then the next he was gone, forever crushing my idyllic world of youthful innocence.

Over time, however, I came to realize that this part of the human condition is as natural as eating or sleeping and one that we need not fear or feel any revulsion against.

If anything, it should spur us on to make the most of our lives while we still have them to enjoy, to be more loving and kind to others and to make every opportunity count no matter what comes our way.

Joy principle thought to ponder and embrace:

The one subject most of us don't talk about until it invades our lives in one form or another is the topic of death. Many of us don't want to think about it because it means the end of something, or someone's life, and we generally don't like to be reminded of those things.

Reality, however, tells us that all living things must eventually die and that includes each of us. Only as we are willing to fully embrace this inevitable truth into our lives can we begin to live life fully each day, consciously making every moment count and tasting just how good, precious and limited are our days here on this planet.

My personal reflection on this principle:

_____

_____

_____

_____

_____

Other Inspirational Thoughts to Ponder and Embrace:

Go forward into this day in a spirit of love, peace, and compassion for every person you meet. You are not superior to anyone else nor are you inferior to anyone else...approaching everyone as an equal allows you to be fully transparent for who you really are without having to pretend to be someone you are not.

Love, joy, peace, kindness, compassion, courage, strength, long-suffering, patience, perseverance, intelligence, insight, intuition, faith-in-God, and hope - the 15 pillars of continuous thought and action throughout the day that keeps one happy and secure within the present moment and all the moments that will follow.

The bottom line is not always the measure of success in a particular endeavor. More often than not, it is the fight and the struggle that one puts into the effort that shapes the inner character for true success to eventually happen.

My past has taught me but it does not hold me; it has opened up doors of knowledge and insight, but it does not define me; it prepares me for the present and the future, but it by itself no longer exists for me.

If you don't worship money, possessions or recognition, but love God and care for the hurts of others, you are on the path to being a free soul.

True success in life isn't simply moving from one accomplishment to another, but more importantly it is that which happens within our character development as we apply ourselves in this journey of constant endeavor toward what we really want.

Do our successful accomplishments make us more humble and appreciative of what we have been blessed with? Or, do they make us more self-centered and arrogant?

Do our setbacks, failures and mistakes teach us wisdom principles to be used for future situations?

Or, do they discourage us and diminish our sense of self-worth and or our capacity to persevere through our difficulties?

The truly successful man or woman is the one who is rich in seeing everything from the perspective of inner growth and knowledge gained whether succeeding or failing in life's pursuits, in whatever form they may take.

For years I have had a metal tag affixed to my keychain that says: "Perfection is the mark for which a champion strives."

I've kept this tag as an inspirational reminder to always try to be the best I can be in whatever I do, while also realizing that perfection is hardly attainable in anything we put our hand to despite our best efforts to try to reach that high mark of achievement.

In recent days I've been thinking that perhaps the word "excellence" might be a more appropriate word to strive towards as it leaves some allowance for life's imperfections, be it from ourselves, others, or even the world we live in.

The scriptures tell us that: "...Whatever is excellent or praiseworthy, think about such things..." Philippians 2:8b-NIV.

Okay, that sounds like something we can each do in our own way and then let the chips fall where they may as we live out our lives in striving to be the best we can be for God, ourselves, others, and the world we live in.

Sometimes in life we read something that strikes a deep chord within us and it changes or enhances something about our values system or how we approach the world and others in general.

Lately I've been pondering the words of Jesus in John 8:32 where he says, "Then you will know the truth and the truth will set you free." (NIV).

Really? Does the power of truth have the capability to set one free and if so, free from what?

One thing I've learned in life that has been of great importance is that we humans have a deep capacity at times to tell ourselves things that may not be entirely correct, or in keeping with the truth and reality of a given situation.

We often do this subconsciously to avoid the pain or difficulty that comes with embracing a circumstance as it truly is. The downside of such an approach however is a disconnect from the truth and the spiritual power that comes with living and accepting things as they genuinely exist.

Truly healthy, joyous living requires us to both see and accept things as they line up with reality and not as we wish them to be.

Whether that circumstance is a good or painful one, the embracing of that truth will always give us clarity, freedom of mind and a deeper understanding into everything that comes our way.

May the truth of our lives and our willingness to always see it as it genuinely is, shine clearly in our spirits as we live out our existence day by day.

Treatise on the Evidence for the Existence of God-Published in The Hamilton Spectator Newspaper-July 21, 2013.

One of the beautiful things about believing in a Creator God in the proper context is the ability to respect other people's opinions that proclaim such a deity does not exist. One may not agree with such a statement but one should be able to say with all graciousness and conviction that each person has the inherent human right to draw their own conclusions about life and its mysterious existence.

Extrapolating some meaning to life from an atheistic perspective I believe is possible, but the question that begs to be answered, "Is that all there is? " Are we humans just here for an incredibly short period of time in relation to the age of our cosmos and then gone?

Could it be perhaps that we are part of some greater design that is now and has been for quite some time moving us onward and upward toward something far beyond our imagining that has been unfolding since life (the manifest order of all things in its' various forms) took hold within the universe?

That being said, no one who has ever lived has been able to prove beyond a reasonable doubt that God does not exist and that no plan (ultimate meaning) lies behind our existence.

One of course can point to several of life's injustices and the many wrongs and forms of evil that surround us on every side and say, " If a loving God existed he would never allow this or that thing to happen, therefore based on this observation alone he cannot possibly exist."

That kind of mind set ultimately of course by its' own set of judgement principles reduces one down to simply living by the five senses that are part of our make-up (hearing, seeing, taste, touch and smell), but is there more to life than just those things alone?

Can something more everlasting possible exist beyond the physical realm? Could it be that it is each generation's ultimate destiny to strive to right all wrongs and to help usher in a kingdom of genuine love and peace that respects the existence of all living things?

I believe upon deeper investigation of the total human condition and the environment in which we live, we can start to find evidence that makes us consider and yes, even accept the existence of a higher being and if we as free-thinking creatures are on some form of trajectory experience that is ultimately leading us to become like the very one who has made us and placed us here each in our own unique human experience.

As we all know, each of us inhabit a human body that has certain drives and needs that have to be satisfied in order to keep us alive such as food, water and air to name a few for example.

However, we also know that one day we are not going to need any of those things and things like them because these bodies we are presently inhabiting are going to die and turn to dust. No big revelation there.

Therefore knowing this, what am I or you to do about keeping ourselves alive in the meantime?

Does my present need or yours for existing mean I (you) can hoard all the food and water for ourselves if that were possible to do, or does it give any of us the right to pollute other people's air just so I can have what I want and not have consideration for the wants and needs of others?

What is it within the altruistic human experience that gives us a sense of ownership and the need to also look out for the needs of others while taking care of our own, or why does it feel so right and fitting that whenever we do things that lift other people or things up to their proper state of being that we sense an incredible deep connection to our true selves and the reason we are ultimately here in the first place?

Could it be that our true selves are more than just self-centered physical and emotional creatures living in a material world and have been called and are yes, even intrinsically designed to bring ourselves and others to a higher state of being that moves us despite our struggles and failures toward a life of total selflessness and giving directed for the welfare of others and our planet in general?

We all know that achieving such a utopian state is so difficult to do at times as we become painfully aware of a competing nature within ourselves that often wars against this kind of high level place of living and acting.

The impending death of beloved international figure Nelson Mandela has given us many reasons in recent days to reflect upon the legacy he is leaving for all of us to consider.

If anyone had the right to be bitter and vengeful because of the wrongs inflicted upon him and his people because of the former apartheid regimes, he did.

Yet upon his release after several years of imprisonment, the deepness of the spirit within the man led him to show an incredible display of national reconciliation, healing and forgiveness for all that had happened so that the best opportunity for peace and prosperity for his nation would go down this road rather than the pathway of bloody recrimination and conflict.

No doubt Mr. Mandela's Christian convictions had a lot to do with how he engaged this terrible oppression in his life for ultimately I believe he knew that doing the right thing often means letting go of those forces that would point us as wounded human creatures in the wrong direction to adversely affect the lives of others.

We also saw this same type of amazing spirit at work in the life of Pope John Paul the 2nd with his near assassination at the hands of Mehmet Ali Agca in 1981 and countless others over the centuries as spiritual man looks beyond all the wrongs of this temporal age and casts a long eye toward the eternal, deep meaningful fulfillment of their human destiny.

Searching out this great meaning of life can indeed be complex at times and so each must pursue their own journey to find it for themselves.

As a believer in a loving, Creator God, that roadmap is firmly in place for me so that I can answer with confidence the three great questions of the ages, "Who am I?" "What am I doing here?" and "Where am I ultimately heading?"

These inquiries have been more than satisfactorily answered for me intellectually, emotionally and spiritually. They find their fulfillment in a grand plan far bigger than ourselves that has been designed by a loving, creative God since the dawn of time and space.

The Ten Rules of Healthy Living-Physically, Emotionally and Spiritually.

1-Eat well.

2-Sleep well.

3-Exercise regularly.

4-Be kind and compassionate toward yourself and others.

5-Be forgiving of yourself and others.

6-Seek more to understand others rather than to be understood.

7-Have faith in God knowing your life is far bigger than what happens in your one lifetime.

8-Find meaning in your work whether it is paid labor, volunteering or home responsibilities.

9-Approach each day with a spirit of love, thankfulness and peace.

10-Learn to accept life on life's terms rather than what you want it to be.

Prayers for Daily Meditation and Focus:

Good morning Father…this is the day that you have made and I am going to rejoice and be glad in it. You are my God and King for you are the Master Father of all things. Nothing is too great that you are not over it all and nothing is too small that you are not in it all. Therefore I will worship you as God and King for you are the Master Father of all things. Amen (so be it).

Life is what it is. I accepted it for what it is and I am at peace with what it is, therefore I will go forward into this day in the power of God to guide and direct my steps. For in this game of life we must remain strong and brave, we must soldier on and never be afraid. For in the end all will be well; victory goes to those who can answer the bell; who can stand up and fight and give it all their might and never give up until all is made right. For the reality of this world is that everything changes and nothing remains the same, except the eternal presence of God and His infinite love for His human creation. Amen.

I rejoice, rejoice in your great power and authority O' God. I relax, relax within your security and your love. I remain, remain within the truths of your words and enjoy your peace. Amen.

I desire the life of joy and peace in whatever comes before me today, therefore I consciously reject all fear, worry, stress and anxiety in all of its various forms. Grant me the insight to see deeply into things as you do O' God and thereby lead me into the eternal ways of bliss and happiness. Amen.

65092731R00032

Made in the USA
Charleston, SC
19 December 2016